start young

Blessings! *Pavelka*

The ABC's and the 123's of
owning a business by the age of six.

JANITA PAVELKA

janitapavelka.com
janitapavelka@gmail.com

Book design by Renee Evans www.reneeevansdesign.com
Editing by Amy Calkins
ISBN: 978-0-9905752-5-2
Printed in the United States of America

dedication

For my parents,
Carrol and Jan Brockel,
who always said I was
"different from my siblings"
and
"the hardest one to raise."
Now you know why.

contents

Introduction

Growing up on the farm, my siblings and I learned from an early age the concept of hard work. We all had to contribute to the family business. At breakfast, we would each be assigned our work details for the day. We were an asset to the farm, and our parents expected us to be industrious, diligent, and grateful for what God had given us. Growing up with that mindset taught me how to be self-reliant, self-confident, and resourceful. I am grateful for my upbringing. It really is true that families who work together thrive together.

My first business idea hatched in third grade. I loved to bake and started making birthday cakes for my classmates. We lived one and a half hours from the closest McDonalds, so it was a treat when we would eat there occasionally. I recycled the Styrofoam Big Mac containers for my cake business, as my tiny cakes fit inside perfectly. I had a "green business" ahead of its time! My love for baking flourished, along with my cake decorating skills, and by the time I was 14 years old I had an "official" cake business. I learned many skills as a farm girl, which helped me make money, first as a child and now as an adult.

As my husband and I raised our four children, we adopted the same expectations. In our home we emphasized teamwork, diligence, gratefulness, and hard work. When our oldest daughter wanted money to put into her savings account so she could win prizes at the local credit union, I asked her, "Well, how are you going to earn money?" She solved her dilemma by setting up lemonade stands.

I asked her the same question when she wanted her first dog. This time, she solved her problem by getting a paper route. Then she asked, "How am I going to feed the dog?" Her answer was to take on a second paper route. This pattern of starting businesses continued until she earned enough business experience and profit to pay for her own clothes, phone, car, gas, insurance, and college expenses.

Children are much more resourceful than we often allow them to be. My advice for parents is simple: Stop giving your children all the answers, and stop fulfilling all of their wants. This will cause them to dig deep and solve the problems they face in life. All four of our kids started their own businesses at the age of six. They started young, and they started small, and their businesses grew alongside them as they matured. Not only that, but they became adept at making decisions, calculating risk, and being future-thinkers.

If you give your children the opportunity to be young entrepreneurs, it will change their lives (and yours!) in many ways. It's OK to leave them with wants in life, because their unmet desires will propel them into higher-level thinking skills. It will give them a reason for learning and help them to be productively engaged with their time to earn their own money. One of Benjamin Franklin's Thirteen Virtues that he practiced by the age of 20 was this: "Industry: Lose no time; be always employed in something useful, cut off all unnecessary actions." Through entrepreneurial experiences, children will grow in wisdom, knowledge, and favor with God and people, and they will fulfill their God-given purpose on this earth starting at an early age.

Gratefully,

Janita Pavelka
July 30, 2016
Oxford, NE

PART 1

The ABCs for Parents

How to Cultivate an Entrepreneurial Mindset in Your Kids

The ABCs in this section will help parents and other adults cultivate an entrepreneurial mindset in themselves, so they can pass it on to their children. This outlook creates fertile soil for seeds of entrepreneurship to be planted in the children's minds. Growth happens through experiential learning, through allowing children to own their own businesses at a young age. It is one thing to talk about being an entrepreneur, but a whole other level of learning happens when you actually live it. When children are immersed in the entrepreneurial mindset and begin to dream, plan, and do the stuff, they become lifelong entrepreneurs. It really does start with you, parents! And it is not that hard. Just start young and start small with your children, one idea at a time.

a

allow

- Allow time in your schedule for your children, as raising adventurous children takes time and attention. Quality and quantity time is needed for strong family bonds, and what better way to do it than discovering how to raise young entrepreneurs? If that is not your bent, then learn right alongside your children. It's a great way to learn (on their level) without feeling foolish. And it gives you a reason to be an entrepreneur yourself! After all, most millionaires have, on average, seven streams of income. Owning your own businesses will get you to that point easier than having seven jobs. If you live it, your children will be more likely to model you.

- Allow your children time in their schedule to be creative and to dream. Create space in your child's schedule to be alone and uninfluenced by peers. Abraham Lincoln spent many hours alone as a child, and he was able to formulate his thoughts about the world and build his convictions. Don't pack your child's schedule with activities, friends, and screen time. Allow your child plenty of down time to dream and create.

- Allow your children to be action-oriented with their dreams as that is how businesses come into being. Dream, plan, and then ACT! Allow them to follow their plans, as all children are created for a specific purpose and have a special future in this world.

b
believe

● Believe that you can succeed at raising young entrepreneurs. You do not need to know all the answers before you start. Just start and enjoy the learning progression with your children. Believe and have faith that God has a special plan for your child's future. Training in entrepreneurship is one of the best gifts you can give them, right after the gift of a faith in God. It will set them up to be industrious, independent thinkers who know how to take action. Our children need to be bold and believe in their ideas. They need to experience success at an early age so they can build on their victories. You, as the parent, don't need to create their success; you just need to set them up for as many experiences as possible.

● Believe in the idea of teaching balance from the beginning. Always take a day of rest from your business during the week. If God needed a day of rest, so do we. Being an entrepreneur is one of the most rewarding professions one can have, but there is no end to the amount of time and work it takes to grow your business. One needs to be self-directed and self-controlled in teaching balance. I remember my dad coming in for dinner on Saturdays and telling our family, "I will be done working in the fields in three hours. Get everything packed in the camper, and we'll go camping." We were motivated. We didn't care if the campground was only five miles from our farm. Or that the woods were infested with ticks and the lake with leeches. We were off the farm and away from our work! Also, we did not do farm work on Sundays.

C
create

- Create an environment where communication is valued and accepted. Allow your children to express their wishes, dreams, fears, emotions, and goals. Create an environment of forgiveness in your household, as we all make mistakes and blow it. What better way to teach it than through hands-on family projects, such as entrepreneurship?

- Create an environment in which it is OK to be competitive in a healthy way. Businesses in the "real world" always have competitors. That's real life! "As iron sharpens iron, so does one [business] sharpen another" (Proverbs 22:17). I was in 4-H for ten years as a child, and I learned many skills through that organization. We had a county and state fair every year where we would enter exhibits that were judged against others' exhibits. The top winners went on to the state fair. Not only did we learn new skills, but it taught us that one had to excel above the competition to win the purple ribbon.

- Most of all, be creative. Take ideas and think outside the box. Come up with new twists on old ideas. Think about solving problems for people. What needs do they have? Be silly and brainstorm, and initially let all ideas be good ideas. The ones that will not work will be sifted out, and the best ideas will rise to the top. Children are very good at brainstorming, being innovative, and being inventive. Let them practice it often.

d
diligent

● Be diligent with your children's plans. Encourage your children to put feet to them and take the risk to act on them. If your kids want to start a lemonade stand on the corner one afternoon, help them do it. Don't worry about all the "what-ifs" first, just start! Lemonade stands were one of the first businesses our children started. Thankfully, they became more professional with their customer service and display, and their product(s) improved.

● Let your children be diligent and determined with their business ideas. Don't let them give up with the first no or refusal. Teach your children how to push through rejection and roadblocks, as the hand of the diligent will rule (see Prov. 12:24).

● Diligence goes hand-in-hand with fluidity. Find your child's interests and cultivate them. Try that business until it reaches a dead end or until a well-thought-out reason for stopping is articulated. Don't let them stop on a whim or on emotions. There will be peaks, plateaus, and valleys in the life of a business. Allow your children time to reevaluate their ownership of their businesses and allow the freedom to move on to the next idea. Businesses will grow with the child. Warren Buffett started out selling pop to his schoolmates on the playground, moved on to selling newspapers, and then pinball machines as a child. As an adult, he has become one of the smartest (and richest) investors in the world.

e

educate

● Educate your children on great customer service. "Sell cheap and tell the truth" was the motto of Russian immigrant Rose Blumkin, builder of the Nebraska Furniture Mart empire, which is now owned by Warren Buffett's Berkshire-Hathaway. Treating customers well is the key to success in business, for without them you wouldn't have a business. As the golden rule says, "Do unto others as you would have them do unto you." What better way to teach children how to be kind and respectful and to treat others well than by owning a business? Practice makes permanent, and they will have many customers with whom they can improve and solidify their ability to take care of the customer's needs. Repeat customers are crucial in a business, along with word-of-mouth advertising.

● Educate your children on the importance of efficiency in their daily schedule and how to avoid squandering their time. Time management learned early in life is a key to reaching goals and learning new skills. Cal Newport's book, So Good They Can't Ignore You: Why Skills Trump Passion in the Quest for Work You Love, explains why skills practiced over time can create income. Being a competitive and successful business owner requires a grip on time. A professional guitar player has said that if he is sitting and watching a movie, he is also playing his guitar. That is time efficiency. Teaching efficiency in time management is essential to being able to own a business and have time for God, school, family, friends, and self.

f
forward thinking

- Forward thinking is the ability to be creative and innovative. It requires hours of mulling over ideas. It also is fun, as your kids can be the first ones on the block to try a new business idea. Mark Twain once said, "Whenever you find yourself on the side of the majority, it is time to pause and reflect." It is good to be unique and to not try to blend in. Innovation works.

- Be a visionary yourself. Or, if that is not a strength of yours, find a mentor for your child who is a visionary— someone who can dream a dream of a different world in the future, someone who can paint a scene for others to appreciate, admire, adhere to, and acquire. One who is imaginative and inspired, original and creative. Forward thinking requires time to research, observe, and think of future trends. Ask: Is my child capable of higher level thinking skills, such as innovation, development, and progressive thought? If they are not to that stage yet, model it for them. Be creative yourself. Always evolve as a parent and be progressive in life.

g
goal-
oriented

● Young entrepreneurs need to be goal-oriented. Doable goals are important for your children. For example, a reasonable goal could be to set up at the Farmer's Market only five times this summer, to sell for two hours, or to sell one bag of seeds. Make goals small, understandable, and attainable for a child. If children achieve small successes as youngsters, it will be easier for them to be motivated and set bigger goals when they are older.

● Goals can also be non-concrete, such as teaching character. Generosity is a character trait, but it is easily imparted through owning a business. Children can have a goal to give back to the community and choose to give 10 percent to a charity. Children can often be self-centered, so it is important to teach them to be generous in their time, talents, and income.

h
hardworking

Through the process of starting and owning a business, children will learn to be hardworking. Everything in life takes hard work and effort, so it is important for children to learn that at an early age. In entrepreneurship, industriousness is a requirement. But, when it is of your children's own making, and they see the visible end results, the hardness of the work is overlooked. Hard work doesn't seem so hard when we know the good fruit it will produce. What an important character trait to learn early in life. It is much more motivating to be told, "Help me stack the cut wood, because you are going to sell it on Saturday," than to be told, "Go stack the wood, because I told you so, and you need to earn your keep. After all, he who doesn't work, neither does he eat." Both approaches require hard work, but one has more incentive attached to it.

Hard work builds self-confidence, worthiness, and pride in a job well done. Another important part of a child's character involves knowing how to work hard to get what they want. Owning a business can give them the incentive they need as they reap the tangible rewards.

i
involve

- Involve children in learning more about their interests. For example, if they are enrolled in guitar lessons, take them to concerts and introduce them to the masters. Immerse them in quality music, so they can emulate the greats. When they become good enough at their craft, then they can give guitar lessons. Immerse them in their craft so they catapult their training.

- Involve your children in community service and giving back to your community. The 10 percent rule is a concrete way to give back to the community. Ideally, community service can be done weekly, as giving of time is also a gift.

- Involve your children in marketing and being on TV, on the Internet, on the radio, in magazines, and in newspapers. The media is your friend, as it is free advertisement for your business. Yes, be wise in regards to their safety, but don't be afraid to contact the media. The world needs hope, and what is better than hearing about young people who are doing good, making it in business, being creative, and giving back to the community. It makes for wonderful news stories, and the world is especially receptive to stories about children.

j
juggle

● Teach your children how to juggle the many aspects of being a business owner by teaching them how to do a job well done by paying attention to the details. This can be hard for some children, if details are not their bent. Some children are big picture kids who have a vision of where they want to go, but the small details of how to get there escape them. If there is a sibling who has opposite strengths, they can be paired together. Bottom line: details need to be noticed by all business owners, regardless of their natural bents.

● Teach your children how to juggle their time between school, business, family, friends, sports, music and dance lessons, chores, church, community activities, and rest. Adding in a business is time-consuming, but manageable. Being their own boss and making money is motivation enough to help them juggle all the responsibilities in their lives. It prepares them well for adulthood.

k
kindle

● Kindle the flame of owning a business by exposing them to successful mentors. Role models can have a powerful influence on our children. Set up opportunities for your child to be exposed to them. Ideally, arrange a formal relationship in which the child has a chance to be mentored by the role model. As they meet regularly, the child will learn business basics and the mindset of an entrepreneur with strong character and ethics.

● Kindle your children's curiosity, interests, and personality bents. The better you know your child, the better you can help and encourage. Continue to expose them to the arts, museums, history, biographies, positive role models, quality literature and words of wisdom, community service, other cultures, and successful businesses that give back. A child who is curious will never stop learning. A life-long learner will be motivated to live life to the fullest, explore the world, and embrace their personality bents. Their mantra will become, "There is a whole world to discover for the rest of my life."

1
look

● Look for other young entrepreneurs, and let your children hear their testimonies. You could start a Young Entrepreneurs Club in your area where families can learn together. "There is wisdom in numbers," so choose to surround your children with other families who have similar mindsets. I started a monthly Family Biz Club that met at the local library. We had 20 to 30 families involved in the nine-month program. The first hour, an entrepreneur spoke to the whole group. The second hour, we split the adults from the children. The adults had a Q & A session with the speaker, and the entrepreneurial mindset was reinforced in the children through age-appropriate learning and activities. We partnered with the local universities and community colleges for our Youth Biz Club Expos. It was a year of explosive growth for young and old alike. The parents were on board, which fueled the children's interests and businesses. I would recommend that program for every community.

● Look for the teachable moments in owning a business, as hands-on learning for children is powerful and lasting. Children can be told information and given wise advice, but the best teacher is experience. If you as the parents do not micro-manage their business, it will be a great training ground where they can make little mistakes early on. Most likely, they will not repeat these mistakes as adults. Sometimes the learning experiences come from the customers, which can be even more impactful.

m

manage

- Manage your records by organizing all income and expenses for tax purposes. Check with your local tax professional on the filing requirements. Check with your state revenue department on business licenses. Children can do most of the footwork for their businesses, but when it comes to legalities, parents need to play a major role, as you are held responsible for the minor in a court of law. But, do not be stymied by fear of what you do not know. Take action, and as a learner, you will grow right along with your child. I'm not saying to do anything illegal. I'm just saying to let your child start small, and when the business takes off, jump through all the hoops. Setting up a lemonade stand on your driveway or the corner of your street will not land you in jail.

- Manage to keep your life in balance so you can be a good role model for your children. To be an entrepreneur, one must work long hours and be driven. Because of this, to be a successful business owner, balance is the key. Focus on the three fundamentals of daily life: good sleep (eight to ten hours per night), whole foods nutrition, and plenty of exercise and movement (preferably outdoors). The value of fresh air, sunshine, and exercise is irreplaceable! Being an entrepreneur is a marathon, as we're in it for the long haul.

n
nourish

- Nourish your children's love of being independent through allowing them to be their own boss. Nourish your children's business growth and leadership by allowing them to make guided decisions about their business. As parents we can guide them, but we should allow them to voice their opinions, think through the decisions, and execute them. Nourish your children's desire to be self-sufficient according to their age. Entrepreneurship strengthens your children's need to make mature decisions and live in the adult world. Continue to foster maturity, which will guide your children's choices.

- Nourish out-of-the-box thinking. If you want children to be creative and innovative, don't make them conform to the standards and images of this world. Foster big thinking, even if that means sheltering your children from too much screen time. Let them spend time in solitude to think, plan, and dream. If they are always "plugged in" or always "scheduled," they will not be able to nourish creative thinking.

- Nourish your own body, mind, and spirit so as to be a good example for your children. Take time daily to meditate on the truth; pray, and give thanks for all things. What we cultivate inside us will determine who we are (see Prov. 23:7). Nourish your physical body with daily exercise, and stimulate your mind by continually learning something new every day. Our spiritual, emotional, and mental prosperity are connected to the prosperity of our health (see 3 John 2).

O

organize

● Organization is imperative in being a successful business owner. Some children are naturally more organized than others, but that doesn't mean there is no hope for the unorganized ones. Instead of nagging your children, let them be motivated to be organized because of their businesses. Organize your children's workspace by de-cluttering it, as they will be more productive if there is less "stuff" in their environment that could distract them. Plus, fewer distractions help with focus, peacefulness, and creativity. Help your children view their environment with a minimalist perspective.

● Organize your children's timeline so they understand what is happening at what day and time. Using a calendar to organize dates, times, and to-do lists work well. At our house, we use Sunday nights to organize for the week with a family meeting. Help organize to-do lists so your children can accomplish small tasks daily. Break everything down into bite-size pieces so your children can feel successful. Organization has a life-long learning curve. We are never too young to start or too old to learn new habits.

P
plan

- Plan to seek the advice of professionals for the technical side of the business. Inquire with the state revenue office, accountants, lawyers, and others who can help answer your questions. Small Business Association (SBA) is a great resource, along with the SCORE (retired businessmen and women) who will be mentors. Our Family Biz Club held an Expo at a local university who invited SCORE members to attend. The retirees met with each young entrepreneur and gave him or her advice. We could not have put a price tag on that type of expertise!

- Plan field trips to visit other entrepreneurs for mentoring, networking, and learning purposes. Field trips are powerful, inspiring, and encouraging. When children can learn first-hand, instead of reading about it in a book or on the Internet, that is best. Children are experiential learners and like to "do" and "see" life. Field trips are impactful and have a long-lasting effect.

q
quit

- As in, don't do it!

- Whatever you do, don't allow your children to quit because they are frustrated or the business is not making money. If the children are not making money, reevaluate the product, the target market, the price, the promotion, and the place in which it is being sold. Allow the children to "retire" the business and find a new one, but do not allow them to quit on a whim. Set an agreed-upon ending for the business and reevaluate. If you need help, reach out to a young entrepreneurship coach who can help you navigate the valleys. If the reason to quit has anything to do with playing video games, that is an absolute no.

- Parents, quit with the "negative Nelly" thinking, comments, and attitudes. If you have some fears, keep them to yourself and take them to God. Your child will fail. Your child will mess up and lose money. At times, your child will have "meltdowns," but whatever you do, don't feed into it. Be positive and self-controlled and picture a special future for your children. Don't let your fears affect the calling on their lives, their purpose on this earth, or the adventures God has planned for them. It is part of your job to picture a special future for your children, always.

r
research

- Research, research, research! Research is extremely important as it keeps you up-to-date on current trends. As an entrepreneur, one has to stay current to spot the next big business opportunity. What are the hot products? Our family would use eBay and Amazon to find out the top sellers. Also, you can use search engines to analyze top searches and innovative new ideas.

- Research competitor's websites, products, and service businesses. Your business will always have competitors, and that is a good thing. If you are the only one with that business idea, there may not be a market for your product or services. Learn from your competitors. Let them spur you on to improving your game. Don't "steal" their ideas, but do emulate them and use them as inspiration.

- Research how to market. There are many ways to sell your products, and you may not be limited to your local market. Use online marketing, and learn from the best. You will find free website services, free photos, free graphic design websites, free email services, free YouTube channels, and free information on the web on how to grow your business. Between YouTube and Google, one can gain a substantial education.

S

start

● Start, as in, start now! Start with one business idea and then go to the next one. Allow your children to start young and start small, and the floodgates of business ideas will snowball. Start with an ordinary idea. It does not have to be a home-run idea to call it a business. View it as a learning experience for the whole family. When your child started to crawl, walk, and talk, there was a learning curve. It is the same with business. Business ideas will always be evolving and growing. But if you get mired in perfectionism, the children will grow up and be gone before they even have a chance to be a young entrepreneur. It is better to start as a young entrepreneur than an old one. The learning curve as an adult is much steeper—much like teaching an adult to play the piano. It is much easier for an adult to be successful if he or she had even a little bit of piano training as a child. It is the same with being an entrepreneur; any business experience is better than no business experience. Something is better than nothing when it comes to youth entrepreneurship.

● Start with assessing needs in your neighborhood. What services do your neighbors need accomplished? Go into business together, and train your children how to mow lawns, rake leaves, wash cars, babysit, run errands, clean houses, housesit, elderly sit, provide doggy daycare, or walk dogs. Neighbors may need their trash cans put back on trash day or weeds pulled in the garden. An elderly neighbor may need help with cleaning out the garage or basement. There are so many service jobs that have minimal costs to start.

t
think

Help your children think through their business step-by-step. Break it down into single thought processes, and chunk it up so it won't be overwhelming. Have them imagine their ideal business in the future, and then start where they are. They have something to offer the world. Babysitting or lawn mowing are not new ideas, but the world needs those services, so start there. Be a thinker, but don't ruminate and never get started. Think as you work, as that is one of the best times to think.

Think about what your children need to give up in order to fit being a young entrepreneur into their schedule. Movie time? Game-playing time? Pool time? Time at the mall? Surfing the web time? Facebook time? Snap chat time? Have them track their activities for one week. Then have them decide which activities they could give up to be successful. Business success is about prioritizing activities and time.

Think about what the neighbors will say, or your friends and family, and then don't think about it. Your family may be different from your friends' families, and that is OK. They will want what you have: children who have the ability to make their own money, who are comfortable with adults, and who know how to plan for the future.

u
understand

● Understand that you, as the adult, won't know all the answers, but learn to seek them out. Be humble enough to learn from others, ask for help, and research what you don't know. This promotes character and perseverance. Plus, it is a great example for your children. Learning is a life-long skill, which will serve you well. Inquiring minds are growing minds. Mentorship, trial and error, and continual self-directed learning will help you reach your goals. As young business owners, children will be motivated to expand these skills, as earning money and gaining independence are attractive to them.

● Understand the significance of a young child owning a business by the age of six and how it will affect their schooling, choices during free time, priorities, future business skills, confidence, and work ethic. Our children did not grow up "normal," and that was and is a plus to their development. They were allowed to make many choices; because of their businesses, they had many decisions to make. They were exposed to public relationships with adults at an early age and had to deliver with professionalism in order to maintain their businesses. They were exposed to learning opportunities through successful mentors, creative ventures, challenging venues, and unique customers, and they had to navigate the relationships and interactions. The impact of being a young entrepreneur will be seen in the immediate, but it will also continue to unfold over their lifetime.

V
value

- Value the learning process. What seems like "play" to you or "peanuts" when a child makes twenty bucks could be life-changing to the child. Never under-estimate the value of experiential learning. Life-long lessons happen through hands-on experiences. Knowledge is needed, but when knowledge is paired with action, it is burned into the memory of the child. Whether it is a successful business or not. Experience is an invaluable teacher.

- Value your children's uniqueness and the ways they are not doing it like everyone else. If everyone else is doing it one way, find another way to do it. Creativity and innovation are a must in life, especially in business. Encourage your children to spend time doing creative activities such as music, art, drama, crafts, writing, designing, dancing, daydreaming, playing in nature, and spending time in solitude. Those experiences are not for naught, as they are opening their minds to new ideas, a fresh perspective, and wisdom from above.

- Value the importance of saving 80 percent of the income as seed money for their future businesses. The 80/10/10 rule works really well for children's businesses, as they have their basic needs covered, so they can roll 80 percent back into their businesses. Then, they can give 10 percent to charity, and the other 10 percent they can spend on themselves, as it is important to "pay" themselves. Any one of these three parts of the equation can be motivating to your child.

W
watch

The definition of watch is to look at or observe closely over a period of time. The more watchful your child is, the deeper the learning experience. That is exactly what we want to happen with young entrepreneurs in their business-building endeavors. Watch and learn from others, especially your competitors. Watch the gurus in your field and emulate them. Watch for opportunities to help younger entrepreneurs and be a good role model.

Watch for balance in your life and your children's lives, as we need to maintain our energy levels. Being an entrepreneur is a marathon, not a sprint, so healthy habits need to be the fundamentals. Be intentional to take a day of rest weekly. Be sure to get sunshine, fresh air, and exercise daily. Eat healthy, whole foods that will feed your brain and strengthen your body. Don't forget sleep, as that is key in making wise decisions and controlling emotions. Our family works hard, but we also play hard. When we go on vacation, we may run a marathon, but we also enjoy the amusement parks. Or we may go snowboarding in the mountains all day, and then enjoy the hot tub and games at night. Balance is the key to avoiding burnout.

X

eXpect

● Expect your child to not be a Bill Gates or Warren Buffet... yet! And don't expect them to get rich overnight. When children make $20 in profit, it is a big deal to them. Don't downplay it. They are on a learning curve. Celebrate their efforts and their fortitude. Realistic expectations of our children are much more encouraging than unrealistic ones. Remember what you were like at that age and how much you could accomplish. How much money did you make? What were you doing to change the world? Make sure your expectations are realistic.

● Expect your children to do lots of the three R's with their businesses. And for us as parents, that is a huge incentive to help them be young entrepreneurs. They may not be motivated in school to get straight A's or finish their homework, but let them have ownership of a business, with the goal of making money, and then watch their motivation soar!

● Expect your children to be ahead of the curve when it comes to knowing their talents, skills, interests, and strengths. It helps us understand our children better when we see them operating in their bent. Watch your children mature before your very eyes, as they will gain skills to operate in the adult world. Expect your child to be seen as a super hero, a rarity, and a good role model because of being a serial entrepreneur.

yearn

● Yearn for excellence. Teach your children to yearn for excellence in their businesses so that they can grow to the next level, be challenged, and desire to learn more and serve others. Of course, your children will not be perfect or fully mature, so be graceful with them. But as they take ownership of their enterprises, you will watch their character flourish. Have them redo their fliers or business cards if there is a typo. Have them redo a task if a client is not satisfied. Excellence (not perfection) can be taught at an early age. Rachel, my oldest daughter, made her signage, and I didn't notice a typo until I was speaking at a conference in front of a room full of people. It read "10% of my profits go to a no-kill human society" instead of "humane society." All I could do was point it out and have a good chuckle.

● Yearn for more. Teach your children to yearn for more in life. Don't settle for mediocrity. Don't settle for just an OK product; encourage them to seek to excel with their product. Yearn for better customer service next time. Yearn for a better pitch and presentation in selling their product or service. Yearn means to crave, desire, and want. Those are all great verbs that motivate us to take action. If your children want more sales next month, help them with a specific marketing plan. If they crave attention, being their own best salesman will get them in front of a crowd. If they desire to go on a trip, have them help earn part of it. One year, when we had a family vacation scheduled to go to Walt Disney World, the children were assigned the task of paying for their own park passes.

Z
zip

Zipping your mouth is an important skill—usually a needed one for us parents. I include myself as I have fallen into this trap many times. I like to give instructions and help with decision making, which my children may interpret as nagging. Sometimes you will have to zip it, especially when you don't agree with a decision your child has made. It is easier for us adults to see the long-term perspective and think it needs to be played out a certain way. But let your child think it through and come to his or her own conclusion. If the consequences are minor, it will serve as a great learning experience. I have allowed my children to set up their own garage sales, only for them to be disappointed in the attendance. I have allowed them to buy 100 shirts wholesale and resell them on eBay at retail prices. At the time, I thought it was quite the risk to take. But my son would often hear his phone "ding" (meaning another purchase) while he was sitting in class at school. He sold almost all of them. And the few he had left he gave to his male classmates as "bro tanks." They loved it and respected his entrepreneurial skills.

PUPPET SHOW

LEMONADE STAND

FLOWER SALES

POPCORN STAND AT THE PARK

DOG SITTING

PART 2

The 123s for Kids

35 Business Ideas that Our Children Owned Over 12 Years

The 123s in this section are the 35 businesses owned in our house over 12 years. Some were successful and sustained longevity, and some were short-lived and not profitable. But, all were great learning experiences. The business ideas contain descriptions and list the valuable lessons learned, irrelevant of the business being profitable or not.

If your children only read one section of the book, this is the section for the children to study, earmark, and use as ideas to start their own businesses.

Children learn by doing, and having real customers is the glue which cements all the learning together. It is also the reason for the child to learn more to become a better business owner. When a customer pays for the product or service, the child is inspired to find more customers or to expand the business, to upgrade it and to excel. Most children need incentive for internal and external growth.

Learning about entrepreneurship and filling our heads with knowledge is important, but it is in the application phase where the life-long learning happens. When a customer compliments a student on a job well done, or when a customer takes a child seriously or becomes a repeat customer, that's when the magic happens. Children bloom, flourish, and grow into a "big dog" when they have positive experiences. Their thought process evolves into, "Yes, I can own my own business. Yes, I can be an entrepreneur. Yes, I can solve problems in the world. Yes, I can fulfill needs. Yes, I have a special purpose in this life."

At every entrepreneurship camp I teach, the goal is always to start a real hands-on business by the end of the camp. It provides motivation for the learning, cements the concepts, and is the tangible reward for the labor. Start young, and start small. Trust me on this one. Every family can be successful, so get to work solving problems and fulfilling needs in the world!

1

PUPPET SHOW

This whole journey started with puppet shows in the next room. Rachel, age 7, Christian, age 5, Hannah, age 3, and Amanya, age 1, scripted, memorized, and choreographed "Ten in the Bed," with Amanya as the "little one" throwing the animals off the top bunk. They charged 25 cents per ticket and used piano studio moms as their captive audience. The moms loved it and were happy to pay the quarter to see the show. At that time, I taught piano in my home to 75 students, and parents were required to attend lessons. "Ah-ha, sitting ducks!", the children thought. They were the customers for many of the children's first ventures. Really, this book could be dedicated to them, as they were an encouraging bunch!

LESSONS LEARNED:

- Children can earn money as preschoolers if they have older siblings or parents who take the lead. All they need is the confidence and forthrightness to go through with the show. Because, of course, cuteness sells!

- Learn one thing well, and you can make money. It takes time to become good at anything. If you have a goal and a team to keep you encouraged, you can endure through all the practices.

- "Captive audiences" are great! The children had an advantage, as their target market happened to be right in their mom's living room! They just needed to be bold enough to ask the parents if they would like to see a puppet show, or buy these products, or need these services.

- Creativity works in selling an idea or yourself. Who doesn't like a sweet children's classic? Or creative kids who take the time to work out the choreography and lines? Creativity sells. People like to be entertained.

2

LEMONADE (AND MORE!) STANDS

The four children took their next venture to the street corner. They set up a table on the sidewalk in front of our house and sold antique belt buckles, carrots and dip, snow cones, lemonade, gourmet popcorn, and juice boxes over a span of two summers. They tried different products until they found the ones that sold best. They also tried different locations and different signage and found corners work better and larger signs work best.

I could keep my eye on them looking out the windows when I wasn't outside. From the very beginning, I was their biggest cheerleader and coach, but I was not the one working the business. I would allow them to make decisions, make mistakes, make amends, and make improvements. It builds confidence in the kiddos, and it fuels the fire for the next venture.

LESSONS LEARNED:

- Location, location, location! And timing, timing, timing! Corners are important, along with fairly busy streets. Pick the "rush hour" in your neighborhood, as traffic flow is important. Even the local policeman stopped for lemonade. Of course the children thought they were breaking some rules and were petrified initially!

- Patience is important, as customers can be sparse. Owning a business is character-building 101. It's great to set up the learning experience and then just watch it unfold before your very eyes. But, when the incentive is there, such as making money, the character traits start to flourish!

- Food products sell better than other items. It is a specific market that need an antique belt buckle found in the old shed. But then again, maybe they were collector items sold for a buck, and someone scored a big bargain! Food sells, but make sure the sign says, "Not made in a state-certified kitchen." Ensure the food items are well made with adult supervision.

- A lemonade stand is a great introduction on how to keep a change box. When pricing products, it is easiest to keep it on the quarter or dollar system, in order for the child to make change with ease. Practicing first with family is important in learning how to make change. They also need to have a secure box, like a fishing tackle box. Hosting lemonade stands in conjunction with family garage sales works well, as the parent is in close proximity to help with the math of change making.

3

FLOWER SALES

Selling flowers, or any type of perennials, is a great business to teach children about profit. Start-up costs are low, and when manual labor is utilized, one can make a nice profit. Rachel, age 8, sold perennials in the neighborhood by pulling them around in her wagon. We dug perennials at our house, or friends' houses, and sold them to homes that needed landscaping. Rachel passed the business down to Amanya at age 6. The girls marketed their perennials to neighbors, mom's friends, and piano studio moms, as well as through group networks. The girls would service their previous customers yearly with offers of different varieties of perennials.

LESSONS LEARNED:

- A nice profit can be made utilizing natural resources, manual labor, and time.

- Neighborhoods are a great place and usually a safe place to sell items. It is important not to "hound" the neighbors, but if they have a need for your products, it would be considered customer service.

- Children can understand customer appeal and charm from an early age. This is not a manipulative tool, but the simple fact that when they look sharp, smile, and use good manners the clients are impressed and more apt to buy their products.

- Networking is key in "grown-up" businesses, along with young people's businesses. Teach your children how to value relationships, give back without expecting something in return, and use networks to get the word out. For children, using Mom and Dad's networks to advertise their products is a bonus. It is especially important to use ethical and professional customer service, as one doesn't want to burn bridges because repeat customers are great, along with word-of-mouth referrals.

- When there is a plethora of perennials to thin out every year, the business it a great "hand-me-down" business for the younger siblings. Basically, it is a gift that keeps on giving. I know of one family who would earn over a $1,000 every year selling their bountiful hostas.

4

FUSED BEADED CRAFTS

Doing arts and crafts is an important part of children's education, as it promotes creativity, dexterity, fine motor skills, hand-eye coordination, and the virtue of patience. When our children were ages 8, 6, 4, and 2, they started making small fusible beaded projects and giving them as gifts to family and friends. Eventually, this evolved into a business as they became adept at the skill and the products were pretty enough to sell. They were satisfied with 50 cents to $1 for the end product. It didn't cover their time, but they were happy, and mama was happy because they were productively engaged with their time.

LESSONS LEARNED:

- Arts and crafts can be a viable product to sell if quality work is done and the right target market is found. Sometimes it would be friends and family who wanted a memento from the child or wanted to encourage the budding entrepreneur. But "mercy purchases" are short-lived, so fulfilling a need is the key in business success. What problem is being solved by this handmade craft?

- What if you don't get paid for your handiwork? Our children learned this lesson the hard way when they made 100 beaded projects for a local school carnival, and then they were "stiffed" by the group's president. Wow, tough lesson to learn. Always get payment promptly, or up front. And always have names and numbers of the purchasers.

- Your investment of time needs to be compensated. Children may not understand this concept initially, but there will be a short learning curve. When they understand their time is money, it will affect the handmade products sold. There is no such thing as "easy" when it comes to earning your own money. That's a myth.

- It's better to give than to receive, as not everything is made for a profit. Teach early the 80/10/10 rule of saving 80 percent of the earnings to reinvest in another business, spending 10 percent on themselves, and giving 10 percent to people or organizations of their choice. This does not relate to only money; it can apply to product also. Giving away product for auctions, fundraisers, bake sales, and charity events is a great way to teach "it is better to give than receive."

GOURMET POPCORN BUSINESS

PavPack Popcorn Sales was born out of our family's love of popcorn. We created unique recipes and a method of making great-tasting gourmet popcorn by experimentation. Our children always had the chance to reevaluate their investment of time, energy, money, and desire for the business. If it had waned and was at a good stopping point, they sold it to their siblings for a negotiated price. They also "tag-teamed" businesses where the child who made the product that week pocketed the profits.

The most successful venue for selling their gourmet popcorn was in the local park at a free weekly summer concert series, as no other vendors were there. All they had to do was obtain a license from City Hall to sell, build an attractive display stand, offer drinks along with the popcorn, and sell to their heart's content. They did post a sign saying, "This product was made in a non-certified kitchen," as per the rules from City Hall.

LESSONS LEARNED:

- Food Products are an investment of time, and time is money, so you have to price your product accordingly to get paid for your time. Making the product and cleaning up can be a daunting and laborious task. It is a great learning lesson building the character traits of commitment, determination, hard work, perseverance, and diligence.

- Teamwork is best in making and selling a product as "many hands make light work." It worked well for our children to work together on businesses so they could divide and conquer tasks and learn teamwork and co-operation. We had a "Family Fund" jar that held the money made from the family businesses, such as selling eggs, chickens, and popcorn, babysitting, building fence, and other family projects.

- Different personalities working together can be a positive, or a negative, depending on the day or the task. There is nothing like a family project to teach collaboration and communication skills. Each personality has different strengths, so it behooved the children to work together, as diversity fortifies the team. The oldest child was the "pusher," the second child was the "let's do this right" coach, the third child was the "creative thinker," and the last child was the "let's have a good time while accomplishing this goal" person.

- Be consistent with attendance, and build your customer loyalty. Don't expect overnight success or to be the most popular business right out of the starting gates.

6

ELDERLY CARE

This business idea started when Rachel and Christian, ages 12 and 10, watched a friend's elderly mother once a week while she was at work. They fed her lunch, played games with her, kept her safe during the day, and provided companionship. It was a gift for both the young and the old. Rachel and Christian didn't have grandparents locally, so the elderly mother was blessed by the sweet children. It was also a great introduction in caring for the elderly, as Rachel went on to obtain her Certified Nursing Assistant's license and worked in a nursing home for four years. This was great preparation for her RN studies at college. Over the years, the children have helped elderly friends clean their yards, do household chores, run errands, and perform musically at nursing homes in the area. Yes, it may be a job, but it teaches the character traits of kindness, gentleness, patience, and warmth with the elderly. It is important to teach the young to respect their elders and care for them.

LESSONS LEARNED:

- Working together with your siblings creates a great team, as your strengths complement each other. Plus, it divides the workload, as it takes a level of maturity and wisdom to care for the elderly.

- The elderly may have many different types of needs such as: physical, mental, social, household, lawn and garden, transportation, errands, paperwork, legal work, and more. Providing an errand service for the elderly has proved successful, along with handyman services.

HANDMADE
JEWELRY

Rachel, Hannah, and Amanya started at young ages making beaded necklaces, bracelets, and earrings according to their artistic talent. They sold them in Mom's piano studio, where there was foot traffic of over 100 people every week. They would make thematic jewelry for the holidays and market them in cute little baskets during the different seasons.

LESSONS LEARNED:

- The caliber of work is important, as you want happy repeat customers. There is a learning curve with making jewelry; it takes patience, fine motor skills, quality craftsmanship, and an artistic eye. Many prototypes need to be conquered before the product is ready to be sold to the public.

- For children, learning a new skill is more important than making money. The more skills children learn and accomplish, the better prepared they will be for life. If they polish and hone their skills, they can exemplify the point of Cal Newport's newest book: So Good They Can't Ignore You: Why Skills Trump Passion in the Quest for Work You Love.

8

A'S CANDY CORNER

Amanya, at age 8, owned A's Candy Corner. She bought unique candy at the store and sold it with a profit margin (emulating the schoolyard days of Warren Buffet). She marketed it to Mom's piano students, who were a captive audience. It was not our favorite business, as she ate too much candy, which affected her health and her profits. Thankfully, it was short-lived. It was one of those "dream businesses" where she had to experience it to believe it really wasn't that great. But, she received lots of lessons learned through the business.

LESSONS LEARNED:

- Don't sell something you like, as you'll eat into your profits. And don't sell something unhealthy, as it will affect your health. Own a business where it is helpful to others and not harmful. Sugar is highly addictive and causes harm to our bodies.

- On the flip side, children will pay money for immediate gratification. Yes, candy does sell well, along with any kind of sweet treats. It will be a popular stand with children where you can make money quickly and easily.

- Amanya sold a desired commodity. It was well-liked and unique candy, in all price ranges, which satisfied all tastes and wallets. One can't argue with that strategy.

9

BABYSITTING

Rachel, Christian, Hannah, and Amanya, ages 10, 8, 6, and 4, started babysitting at a young age as they baby-sat in our home. Mom was there to supervise and add the temporary child(ren) to the daily schedule. Children get tired of babysitting all day long, so they need reinforcements. Working as a team was a great combination, as they would tag-team when they needed a break. The children made money and were glad to be able to put it into the Family Fund account, where they were saving for Walt Disney World park passes.

LESSONS LEARNED:

- Some (temporary) children fit into the family routine better than others. Be aware of the watched child's needs, personality, and if it is a good fit for your family's routine.

- Getting paid is better than bartering for the services. Children would rather have money. Bartering as payment may be a complicated concept for younger children to understand.

- Babysitting as a family is needed, as the children will need breaks and benefit from taking turns. Fitting the temporary child into the usual daily routine is much easier than making the day revolve around the visiting child. For example, the child can be taken on the paper route, or help fold papers, or help with daily chores, or learn skills right alongside your own children.

10

RACHEL'S DOG SERVICES

Rachel, at age 8, loved dogs. We dog sat for friends' dogs before we had our own dog. It gave her experience, skills, and an idea of dog ownership. She saved her newspaper carrier money to buy Dustin, her first dog. She branched out from dog sitting to doggie daycare and dog watching at clients' homes. She found there was a market for doggie daycare and dog sitting while the owners were at work or on vacation. She would get paid $10–15 per day for dog sitting. It was a no-brainer for her. Rachel would take the dogs on a walk while she delivered her paper routes in the afternoons, thus learning the valuable skill of compounding her time. She was getting paid to do her paper routes and getting paid to care for the dogs.

LESSONS LEARNED:

- Service businesses pay well. If you take excellent care of peoples' dogs, they will pay you well. People like their dogs, and they have no problem spending money on them. If you deliver over-and-above service, clients may even tip you!

- You can earn money from your skills. Rachel owned her own dog and knew how to care for him, so she felt skilled enough to serve other clients and their dogs. The more skills a child can learn, the better. It really is not about passion in starting a business. It is about getting really good at a skill and marketing it.

- Sometimes one is not prepared for rapid business growth. The business grew so quickly; Rachel would have small dogs on certain days and large dogs on opposite days. It is important the dogs are socialized and get along well with people and other dogs. Rapid business growth is a good problem to have. It makes the owner be a creative problem solver.

- Dogs need to be up-to-date on vaccinations. Also check the local ordinances regarding the laws on number of dogs in a home. It is better to check than find out the hard way, with the officials knocking on your door.

GARAGE SALES

I love going to garage sales and looking for items I need, but I detest hosting my own. But the children thought they could make money selling their "stuff," so they held their own garage sales in our driveway. They cleaned out books, toys, household items, and clothes to sell. They asked friends to bring over items to make it a larger sale. They posted signs around the neighborhood and ads on social media to get more traffic. Traffic and location is highly important in holding a garage sale. None of their garage sales drew large crowds or made a huge profit. Our house was not located on a busy street, and it was off the beaten path.

LESSONS LEARNED:

- A garage sale needs lots of "cool stuff" listed. People are looking for collector or popular items and unique or useable items. If it is old, torn, or well-used, give it away to a charity. People don't want to buy junk. Or have a free box. People like free.

- Host the garage sale with friends. People will drive by and look to see if it is worth their time to stop and shop. Make sure you have enough items to attract customers. A two or three household garage sale will fill the garage and driveway with items that are attractive to potential customers.

- Garage Sales take a lot of preparation time for an unknown and unpredictable return on investment (ROI). One can never predict if it will be a $1,000, $100, or $10 sale. It's a great learning lesson for the children. As I tell my children, "Just do your best and let God take care of the rest."

- Garage sales are a perfect time for your children to sell their own products or advertise their own service businesses. It is a safe environment where the parents can monitor closely. Hopefully the foot traffic will be there, and the children have a positive experience. Young children, even preschoolers, can work a table to sell lemonade and baked goods under a watchful eye.

12

STARFISH SOAP CO.

Christian, at age 10, started Starfish Soap Co. that sold handmade organic soap. He named it Starfish Soap Co., as he gave ten percent of his profits to Starfish Ministry, which fed the homeless in downtown Omaha. Every Sunday our friends would organize a meal, including hygiene products and clothing giveaway, for the people in need. We helped many times and formed relationships with the homeless people. Christian sold the soap for four years until he felt like he outgrew the business as a 14-year-old young man. He also found that the soap sold better in the city than it did in rural areas, as we moved to the farm when he was 12 years old.

LESSONS LEARNED:

- Unique niche products sell well in the cities. Christian found that in rural areas he had to lower his prices. He also found that money flowed freer in the cities, as the population base and possibly higher paying jobs are located there.

- Buying quality products wholesale and selling them retail is a great way to start your own business and build an excellent reputation. It guarantees quality and consistency with the merchandise.

- Being able to sell your product is a huge plus, as salesmanship is needed in every business. A perfect business pitch is important. All of our children had a pitch memorized for their businesses. People may buy it just because you are a good salesman (and cute to boot!).

- Giving back benefits others, but the biggest benefit is personal character growth. Making money with your business is a necessity (or else your business wouldn't exist) but character tops the bankroll any day. The family who founded Starfish Ministries had an instant bond with this young boy who would name his business after their charity and faithfully donate 10 percent off the top. The mentorship has only grown over the last ten years, as Christian recently went on a missions trip to Jamaica with this family. Yes, this book is about creating young entrepreneurs, but even more important is creating young people who are philanthropists.

13

HANNAH'S SPARKLING CANDLES

Hannah, at age 8, bought beeswax sheets from Franchild.com and rolled her own candles. Hannah is very artsy and liked to make her own products. Her finished goods were unique and pretty, but sold only seasonally. They were not a good product for summer farmers markets, as they melted in the heat. She rolled the sheets of beeswax into candles with wicks placed in the middle.

LESSONS LEARNED:

- Unique, handmade products are great to market as artisan creations. They need the right target market in attendance. These candles were marketed to women who like custom-made handiwork.

- Candles are seasonal and not a good product for summer farmers markets, as they melt. Outdoor venues can bring all the challenges of the elements. Again, it is character-building for children to manage non-ideal conditions; it builds resilience and flexibility.

- Some personalities are geared for sales, and some are geared for making the products. Generally, extroverts are more comfortable as salesman, but all children need to be the best salesman for their business, regardless of personality type. It helps if most children have a script and can practice at home before encountering the public. As much as possible, set your child up for success initially, which will build their confidence. When confidence grows, so does the ability to sell in any setting or with any competitors.

14

A'S AWESOME JEWELRY

Amanya, at age 6, bought American-made jewelry wholesale from Franchild.com and sold it wholesale at farmers markets. Sometimes jewelry sells well, but you need to have wholesale prices low enough in order to make a profit at retail prices. Amanya had a tri-fold board we painted pink and used to display the jewelry. She was able to sell one batch of jewelry, and we never ordered again. She decided the jewelry was too expensive for her to buy wholesale and try to sell it retail. In our house, we valued experiential learning and allowed the child to make most of their choices. It helped with their higher-level thinking skills, future planning, and evaluation skills.

LESSONS LEARNED:

- The product needs to be unique. The child and teen's jewelry market is flooded with options. What sets your merchandise apart? Why would they buy yours and not the jewelry at the mall?

- The product needs to have a lower wholesale price in order to make a profit. This is a great lesson for children. Can their target market sustain higher price points? What are the price points in their area? Answers lead to market research on competitive pricing

- The jewelry needs to be well made. This is a given. Only sell well-crafted products. If you wouldn't buy it, why would you expect your customer to?

15

YO-YO BALLOONS

This was another one of my favorite businesses. It was a joy for all as the kiddos were happy with the toy, the parents were happy that their children were happy, and my children were happy to have money in their pockets quickly and easily. All the children were involved in this enterprise, as it was quick and easy moneymaker. At the recommendation from another family, we jumped into this idea, cold turkey and with both feet. We ordered the balloons and supplies off the Internet, with minimal costs involved. The children assembled the balloons themselves. The kit came with a pump, stand, and easy-to-follow directions. We sold them at street fairs, farmers markets, and other festive gatherings where there were families with children. The Pavelka children walked around demonstrating the toy. Playing with the product produced more sales.

LESSONS LEARNED:

- The children were motivated and needed little supervision in assembling. They were motivated because the product came together so quickly and easily, unlike washing dishes, which is a chore!

- The right venue is key. A festival or carnival atmosphere is best, as parents will spend a buck on a toy for a child. Always think about your target market and where there is a lot of foot traffic. One dollar for a toy that has a short learning curve and mesmerizes the child is a winner!

16

R'S GIFT BASKET'S

Rachel created this business herself, because she thought thematic baskets for men, women, and children would sell. She bought a variety of thematic items and made an attractive arrangement in a basket. She covered the baskets with cellophane to look pretty and sold them at the business expos we held on college campuses. Rachel researched to find what her target market spent their money on.

LESSONS LEARNED:

- You need the right venue in order to sell the baskets. Women are more apt to be interested in them than men or children, as they are usually the gift givers in the household.

- Watch the price on the items you purchase, as you need to make a profit on the basket. If the items you buy have no room for a mark-up, you won't make much profit on the product.

- If you purchase items at a garage sale or thrift store to resell, make sure they are brand new items. This lesson was learned the hard way, as money had to be refunded to an unhappy customer, who happened to be a college business professor. It is hard to hear negative feedback and face rejection, but humility and honesty rule in business. Offer a refund, along with a sincere apology, and learn from your mistakes. That mistake won't be repeated again.

17

HANNAH'S SPA ITEMS

Hannah, at age 10, needed a new business idea. We met a woman who created spa products and were impressed with the quality. She was a perfectionist and a master chemist, but not much of a marketer. Our forte was marketing, so we teamed up with her to help sell her spa items. They were superior products, and in the right market would sell well. Hannah chose to sell the handmade organic soaps, body lotions, runner's foot balm, and eye pillows. She sold them at expos and farmers markets, as her target market was women who like to pamper themselves. We discovered they sold better in the city than in the rural areas due to the price points. We also found that we chose too many products to sell and invested in too much inventory for Hannah to manage. She also did not make a profit on this business, as she had excess inventory leftover.

LESSONS LEARNED:

- Purchasing quality products wholesale for children to sell retail can be a great business model. Children may not be capable of producing the same type of excellent products as adults.

- When selling high-end products, make sure you test the market before investing in too much inventory. Be careful if the wholesale price is too high, as the profit margin may be slim in the retail price. Buy sample packs of new products in order to test the market.

- If a child becomes discouraged with low sales, teach them about perseverance and patience. Not every product is going to fly off the shelves. Sometimes it depends on the salesmanship ability of the entrepreneur. Other reasons for poor sales may include: the target market is absent, people are hot or tired, the child is being timid in asking for the sale, or the display is not attractive.

- Watching the product being made is helpful when the child markets it, as knowledge makes for a more powerful sales pitch. The child needs to know all the benefits and features of a product to be able to sell well.

18

A'S SUNFLOWER SEED CO.

Amanya, at age 7, wanted another business idea, so we decided on Wild Dutchman Sunflower Seeds from South Dakota. The seeds are locally grown, and the father-son business built the manufacturing plant right on their farm, which is ten miles north of Amanya's grandparents' farm. Amanya was the first and only distributor of Wild Dutchman Sunflower Seeds in our state at that time. She buys them wholesale and sells them with a mark-up to 14 local stores in our area. She also sells them at farmers markets, concession stands, and as fundraisers. Sales have grown over the years, to the point that we have them directly shipped to the store for some accounts. It has stood the test of time because there is a demand for the product and there is a profit with minimal time invested.

LESSONS LEARNED:

- Teach your child how to use Excel spread sheets and invoices. It is a great skill to know. Any computer training as a child will serve them well in life. Most kids like to be on the computer, so it might as well be to make money!

- Take a tour of the manufacturing plant so the child has first-hand knowledge of the business. Not only is it educational, but also it plants seeds of bigger business ideas for the future. Adult entrepreneurs serve as role models and mentors and can plant entrepreneurial seeds in fertile soil.

- Find a product that is not available in your area and become the first (and only?) distributor in your area. But only if there is a need and a market to sell your product. Once people taste the Wild Dutchman sunflower seeds, it is really hard for them to go back to the salty and MSG-filled other sunflower seeds on the market.

- Let the child do the math so they realize practical math is needed and important as a business owner. So many students have a block towards math. I know my girls did in school. But, when they are working on their own businesses, math is no problem. Real-life learning early is the key to life-long learning.

- Make sure you like the product you sell. A child is more fired up if they use their product. They can speak honestly about it as personal stories help sell the goods.

19

EVERY GIRLZ DREAM JEWELRY CO.

Rachel, at age 13, had her ears pierced for her birthday, which turned her on to the world of earrings. One day while researching on the Internet, she spied some gorgeous and unique jewelry and promptly imported a sample pack. The Incan artisans in the Andes Mountains handcrafted the Peruvian stone and Murano glass jewelry. Rachel sold the first sample pack in one day at the state fair, so she then placed another larger order. Rachel even had females buying the jewelry from her and starting their own businesses. The product sold at consignment shops, expos, farmers markets, online, and by word-of-mouth. The jewelry was modestly priced; therefore, it was a good seller with females of all ages. It was a great business for Rachel, as she was able to support the Incan artisans and give donations to the indigenous children monthly.

LESSONS LEARNED:

- Importing jewelry helps the artisans of that country. Yes, business is about making a profit, but it also helps to have an altruistic element. Teaching children about the culture and artisans is important, as the artisans need to make a decent living.

- When importing jewelry directly from the artisans, the wholesale prices can be kept low, therefore making your return on investment (ROI) highly profitable. Even in a sluggish economy, females will buy reasonably-priced jewelry.

- When introducing new products into the marketplace, it is wise to buy a sample pack to test the market, as it is easier to manage than one where the loss is devastating. It is a valuable skill for the young person to learn how to take calculated risks early in life.

- Importing a unique product drew the attention of other female entrepreneurs who wanted to sell the jewelry. Rachel sold the jewelry wholesale (with a mark-up) to four other females, and they were able to start their own cottage businesses.

- This was by far the most successful business for Rachel. This business landed Rachel on radio and TV and in newspapers, magazines, books, and videos. It also won her a spot as a workshop and convention speaker and enabled her to win local, state, and national entrepreneurship awards. It definitely had longevity and is still in operation today, only on a smaller scale.

20

DOOR-TO-DOOR
DISTRIBUTION
SERVICES

All four children were hired numerous times to hang business and campaign flyers on doorknobs, to place phone books on porches, and to distribute flyers during a parade. The challenge was to divide and conquer the neighborhoods to get the job done as quickly as possible.

LESSONS LEARNED:

- Working together as a team can be more profitable and fun. We would set a goal and work to meet, or beat, that goal.

- Bid the job high enough to make it worth your time. If four or five people divide the payment, make sure it is agreeable for all. Sometimes we would put the payment in our Family Fund jar and use it for family activities or vacations.

- If you are hired to do two distribution jobs at once, that means twice the profit. The ideal situation is if you can compound your time and get paid double. For example, if you have a paper route, you can deliver the fliers while you deliver the newspapers.

- Bonus: You can get exercise and get paid at the same time!

21

HANNAH'S CARDS
AND STATIONERY

Hannah is artistic and liked to create her own products to sell. The products took longer to generate, but it taught her patience and perseverance. If you have an artist in your family, cards and stationery are a great place to start. They are consumable, and people need cards for different occasions. Find pretty stock paper with matching envelopes and mass produce the best designs. Drawing or painting each one individually is not necessary with the quality of copiers we use today. If they are drawn individually, be sure to charge enough to account for their time.

LESSONS LEARNED:

- Let the artistic children create their own products, as they will be more invested in the salesmanship. When Hannah believed in her product, she was a tenacious salesman. If your artist is an introvert, teach them a sales pitch so they know what to say to potential customers. Partnering with a sibling who is not an extrovert also works well. One sibling can create the product, and one can sell the product.

- The artists can draw in their niche, whether it is horses, birds, dogs, or comic book characters. An autistic girl who spends hours making cute comic book scenes did the illustrations for this book. I think she needs to sell her cherubic characters as Emojis to Facebook.

22

HOMEMADE FOOD PRODUCTS

The children sold their baked goods at farmers markets, Entrepreneurship Expos, to friends, and to other customers. These recipes were tried and true, our favorites, and received compliments when served to others. The granola and the apple pockets were healthy alternatives to the ones found on the supermarket shelves. The challah was a family favorite that is served at Friday night meals. The fruit leather was made from excess fruit on our farm. We marketed our products as homemade, organic, made with butter, local honey, and eggs. If the child likes to bake, this is a great business, as food usually sells. Find a venue where the food does not need to be made in a state certified kitchen, and post a sign stating that fact. But, state certified kitchens might be easier to find than one thinks. Check with local churches, community colleges, or even restaurants. Don't let the laws defeat you before you even start. Imagine the business you would like to own and then create it; keep asking and pursuing avenues until you can make it happen.

LESSONS LEARNED:

- Let your child experiment in the kitchen until they find the winning recipe. Cooking involves math and science, especially when you experiment with recipes. If they like to discover, the kitchen is a great place for chemistry, and the bonus is that you get to eat your concoctions.

- If the product and the child are a good fit, magic happens, and the child takes off with marketing creativity, motivation, diligence, organization, and energy. It's a fascinating process. And the opposite is also true. If the product and the child are not a good fit, it's really hard for children to "fake it." Adults may be able to "fake it till you make it," but children usually cannot.

- It can take a while to build a clientele when selling in a new venue. When we came on the scene at our local farmers market, there was a woman who had been there for 11 years and had customers lined up at her table. The children were discouraged initially, but it was a great character-building experience for the children to be patient and persistent, and eventually it paid off.

- For the child, the worst part of baking can be the cleanup. There are many dishes to wash, and dry, and it needs to be done over and over again.

23

HANNAH'S TOFFEE

One holiday season we discovered a successful business with high quality, high-end toffee. The artisan product was made near the grandparents' farm, but not sold in our area. So another business idea sprung to life. What if someone were to invest in wholesale toffee and market the high-end product to financial service offices in our area for holiday gifts? After all, it was listed as one of the select gifts on the website. Hannah decided to invest in the handmade product and did cold calls in a local city of 30,000 people. She targeted financial service offices who might want to give it as gifts to their clients. After facing many no's in a row, she became discouraged and lost her motivation to continue knocking on doors. The investment wasn't a moneymaker, as the marketing plan was abandoned, but the melt-in-your-mouth toffee sure was a treat for us to eat…literally eating our profits!

LESSONS LEARNED:

- Make sure the timing and the requirements of the marketing plan works for the child, as cold calling is not easy and requires a certain personality to execute. Networking was utilized, but Momma doesn't have networks everywhere!

- Don't eat your profit, unless it is as a last resort, as the high-end gifts cost a bundle wholesale. They were also given as nice gifts to people, so it was part of her 10 percent of giving back to the community.

- Thankfully it was a small quantity, and we were able to test the market, so it was a calculated risk with a small loss in the big picture of life.

- Since the toffee was a high-quality product, the wholesale price point was higher than the average candy one would buy in a store. When factoring in the mark-up for the retail price, it had to be marketed as a luxury product, something extravagant, which narrows the market of who is willing to spend that type of money on their clients. I still think the target market was accurate, but it was just not the right timing to make the sales.

24

PAVPACK ACRES PUPPIES

Rachel had an affinity for dogs early on, so when she was 10 years old, she used her paper route money to buy a chocolate lab named Dustin. After four years of taking care of Dustin and other people's dogs, Rachel started a small kennel and raised Morkies and Malteses. It required much study and training to become a quality breeder. She sought out a knowledgeable breeder as a mentor and used a local vet for her well checks. She researched online on how to register her puppies with national accreditations and was a whiz at marketing. Both she and Christian would make sweet puppy movies, take adorable puppy photos, and post them online. People loved them! They built free websites, created YouTube channels, updated Facebook pages, and sold 70 percent of their puppies online. Marketing is at the heart of any business' success, and those two were naturals. In fact, they were asked to do marketing for other kennel owners, which was another business opportunity!

LESSONS LEARNED:

- There is a learning curve, so study beforehand to show yourself approved. It is definitely a family affair, as it takes many hours to care for the dogs and litters, to market, and to deliver the puppies. The whole family has to agree to this business idea, as it even affects family vacations, since a person will need to be hired to do the chores.

- The child needs a mentor if you are not familiar with the kennel business. There were families in our area that were also breeders, and the children spent many hours learning from them. Mentorship and apprenticeships are imperative in starting this type of business!

- Marketing and selling the puppies online is the key to successful sales and getting the price you want. Online sales need to have higher price tags, as most likely the puppy will need to be shipped and delivery arranged.

- Cleaning is a constant chore. It is not fun, glamorous, or the moneymaker, but it is necessary due to sanitation laws and health for the dogs and puppies. It teaches a work ethic, cleanliness, stewardship, organization, and diligence—all great character qualities that will serve you well in life.

- Money can be made in breeding dogs, but you need to know your breed well, retain the integrity, and identify which dogs are the hot sellers. And of course, be a quality, conscientious, and meticulous breeder in caring for the dogs, complying with the rules, and registering with the necessary agencies.

25

FARM BUSINESSES

We moved from the city to a rural area and bought "Old MacDonald's Farm" so we could raise animals, grow gardens, and have productive ground. Hannah boarded horses and the profit went right into hay for her three horses. All four children raised meat goats. The kidding process was their absolute favorite part. Their least favorite was the long-term investment and the unpredictable losses with the herd. At one point we owned 125 laying hens, ducks, and one turkey. The eggs sold well, but chickens do not lay eggs year-round. We also raised 175 broilers (meat birds) that provided meat for three families. Grass-fed beef has been our favorite meat thus far. The taste and the health benefits have us hooked on it. We sell (or give away) excess produce and herbs from our garden. The 150 grape vines that we planted didn't survive in our soil, along with the 27 fruit trees. No matter what project we wanted to undertake, we had to research, ask the experts, and learn from experience. You feel the failures in your pocketbook and in your heart.

LESSONS LEARNED:

- Setting up a farm costs money, and lots of it! Tractors and implements, pick-up truck and trailers, four-wheelers and helmets, tillers, mowers, a log splitter, shop tools, kennels, pens, fences, sprinklers, livestock, flocks, herds, pets, cages, hay, feed, seed, vet bills, etc. It is an unending list. Our realtor warned us, but us "city folk" moving to the country were pretty "green" about it all. I was raised on a farm, but it was many years ago when I left the farm for the city lights.

- Owning horses can be expensive. They require hay in the non-pasturing months. In the summer months, they graze in our pasture. They have vet needs, hoof care, supplements, and tack needs. Boarding horses can be a moneymaker, but it is a big responsibility. Every horse owner has their own opinions about caring for their horses.

- Baby goats (kidding) is educational and a rewarding venture. Every child needs to experience the birth process. The mama goats are much less intimidating than mama cows, and the kids come out vigorous and ready to stand almost immediately. If the birth goes as planned, it is a sweet experience.

- Selling eggs will not put you on easy street. But, having your own "egg money" is important, as my grandmas used to say. We put our "egg money" into a jar and took it directly to the feed store to buy feed. We did not see a profit with eggs, and we had to buy our feed at retail prices.

26

CHRISTIAN'S
GUITAR STUDIO

Christian started with piano at the age of four and guitar at the age of six. He is a natural teacher and relates well to people. At the age of 14, he started his own guitar studio and taught guitar classes, which compounded his time and bottom line. If your child excels at a musical instrument, they can teach lessons and earn a nice income. Group lessons yielded $60 per hour, which is great pay for a teenager.

LESSONS LEARNED:

- It is easier if teaching is an innate skill. If it is not a natural skill for the teacher, it can be a frustrating experience for both the teacher and the students.

- No matter how good the teacher, some children will not learn to play, and it usually has to do with the support at home or lack of practice.

- If you are teaching an instrument, you need to be taking lessons yourself and growing as a musician.

- Patience is necessary for a teacher, because each student learns differently.

- Don't limit your studio's target market just to children. Adults make great students also. Now they may have the time and income to take lessons they missed out on as children.

27

EBAY SALES

EBay sales are great for the child who is detail- and research-oriented, good at customer service, and analytical. Christian started his eBay business after discovering hot selling items on eBay. He sold clothes, sports items, books, electronics, and collectibles. He also sold for other people and organizations on a commission basis.

LESSONS LEARNED:

- Research to find the hot items and ride the trends. Christian found that name brand sportswear sold well, so he specialized in that area. Take clear, detail-oriented pictures, as customers want full disclosure.

- Emulate the successful sellers and do what they are doing. Christian had an eBay mentor who helped him get started in the business and even gave him leftover shipping supplies. Scour clearance items, garage sales, and thrift stores for new or like-new bargains that you can resell. Watch out for shipping costs, as it can cut into your profits.

- Don't start the bid out too low. Be patient and re-list it at another time. In the beginning there is a learning curve, so don't start your learning curve with the big-ticket items. Christian lost money on his first few items, as he started with collectibles. Someone received a good deal on Johnny West, but it's okay; those are easier lessons to learn as a child than as an adult, as the financial loss may be greater in adulthood.

28

MARSHMALLOW GUNS

This business idea was a new twist on an old idea. Marshmallow guns made out of PVC have been around for a while, but Christian changed the design and covered them with duct tape. They sell well at street fairs, festivals, and carnivals, where there are lots of families. The guns are made out of pvc, plumbing connector pieces, and duct tape. The new twist on the old idea is the themed duct tape, black connector pieces, and pistol design. At one street fair, more guns had to be made for the next day, as they sold out after the first day.

LESSONS LEARNED:

- Boys are generally the target market, but some girls like them too, along with dads. Usually the guns are bought in pairs so they can have their marshmallow wars.

- Have a marshmallow war around your booth to attract customers. Include marshmallows with the gun as an incentive to buy. Don't eat the ammunition, as you will eat up your profits.

- Sometimes the new buyers had to be taught how to use the guns. Remember, it's all about great customer service.

- Christian did well with this business and then sold it to his sister Amanya, who still owns it.

29

BRING ON THE BLING

Rachel owned her jewelry company for three years before bringing on a partner. They expanded the inventory and renamed it Bring on the Bling. They added four new jewelry lines and offered purses and hair accessories. Bringing on a partner adds energy, new ideas, and capital to your business, but it also requires clear communication. Each partner has strengths and talents that can be utilized constructively. Sales can be doubled, tripled, or quadrupled, but it also means being accountable, checking in frequently with the other person, and splitting the income and expenses.

LESSONS LEARNED:

- Make sure the communication is clear and both partners have mutual understanding of the roles and goals in the business. New energy, ideas, and products come with a partner. Strengths can be utilized in a partnership and roles divided according to personalities.

- Inventory was sold at county fairs, town festivals, street fairs, Fourth of July celebrations, storefronts such as hair or nail salons, state fair, the National 4-H convention, and in consignment stores.

SNOWFLAKE RANCH KENNELS

Christian fell in love with Newfoundland dogs after purchasing Lexie during his first summer on the farm. The breed is smart, sweet, and full of personality. He eventually purchased an existing kennel from a retiring breeder. He cared for them daily and paid for all expenses, such as feed, shots, grooming, vitamins, vet check-ups, and transportation. Christian was able to sell the puppies locally and online, which involved shipping them to other parts of the country or taking road trips with a van full of puppies.

LESSONS LEARNED:

- Marketing online is invaluable as people love to watch puppy videos. Cute puppy pictures and videos attracted hundreds of potential buyers. Also, names make a difference. If you give them popular names that are trending online, they will come up in the search engines, which help with sales. Keeping current with the online world is imperative in marketing puppies.

- Christian found out that being able to market the puppies on his own was more profitable than going through a third party, such as a puppy broker, pet store, or online website which took a percentage of the sales.

- He also realized the marketing skills he was learning through his YouTube channel, website, Facebook pages, Instagram, and Twitter accounts were profitable skills for the future. Veteran kennel owners asked him to do their marketing. Marketable marketing skills = another business option.

- Christian is a researcher, which served him well in this business. He learned about vaccination requirements and usually administered his own. He had a relationship with the local vet for puppy checks and care of his adult dogs. He researched the airlines' shipping requirements, as many of his dogs were shipped. He was aware of the state requirements for dog breeders. And most importantly, he found local breeders who were willing to mentor him.

31

PERUVIAN IMPORTS

Rachel and Christian imported items directly from Peru through a Peruvian importer. They found items online they liked and contacted the distributor directly. The two built a trusting relationship with the importer and ordered through him for years. Rachel and Christian imported jewelry and accessories, finger puppets, woolen hats, and scarves. It is a given that the parents will be involved in all phases of the child's businesses. Safety was used in the use of the internet, business transactions, and all communications.

LESSONS LEARNED:

- It's important to buy a sampling of imported goods and test the market to see if they are a hit with your target market.

- A business relationship can be built on the Internet, and even youth can import items.

- It's okay to bargain with an adult businessperson. Bargaining skills are important in business. "You can do better than that, can't you?"

- Some products are seasonal, and some products are only "hot sellers" for a time. It is wise to have multiple outlets for selling your products in case one venue is not producing as planned.

- Think unique. Think different. Think outside of the big box store mentality. This is important when ordering your items and when thinking about venues to sell your products.

32

HAIR FEATHERS

Observation of current trends is an important skill to have when thinking of new business ideas. Rachel spotted the new trend, ordered the supplies, and taught herself how to apply hair feathers by watching YouTube videos. She rode the trend by offering the service at community gatherings where there were many teen and tween girls. It was a short-lived business, due to it being a trend, yet she made money and gained another skill.

LESSONS LEARNED:

- YouTube is a great teacher of many marketable skills.

- As an entrepreneur, one needs to be an observer of current culture and know what is "cool" and ride the trends, within bounds.

- Importing the necessary items is better for your bottom line than buying retail.

- Cleaning combs and tools between customers is of utmost importance, so as not to spread lice and other worrisome plagues.

- This business lasted two summers. By the time it was passed down to her sister, it was out of style.

- This type of skill is one that can be used to bless other girls. It can be used at a charity event, a makeover event, or to build self-esteem in girls. Giving back to the community needs to become second nature to young entrepreneurs.

33

NETWORK MARKETING

When network marketing is mentioned as a business opportunity, many people have preconceived notions. It can be met with skepticism, disdain, and prejudices. Some of the best-known companies in America, including Avon, Mary Kay Cosmetics, and Tupperware, fall under the network-marketing umbrella. If they are built on that structure, it is reasonable to think that we can be open to other legitimate companies built on the same principles.

Christian and Hannah joined a discount travel club the day they turned 18. They set goals and work on personal development through exercise, prayer, reading character-building books, and relationships with people. They have taken trips with the company and can testify about the quality products offered. Yes, network marketing can be controversial, but when personal growth and development is obvious, I bank on "you shall know them by their fruits."

LESSONS LEARNED:

- It takes guts to be in a network marketing business, as most people have a strong opinion regarding it.

- Meeting with people you know (or don't know) can be scary and intimidating. One needs to manage emotions and not take rejection personally.

- It takes a daily practice of intentional little habits that add up to big changes over time. Ten minutes do make a difference. If the "teams" offer support and accountability, personal development is bound to happen.

- Sometimes it is a lonely road to think differently than mainstream society. This is why we need to fortify our minds and continually cast a vision for our lives. It builds confidence, which a person needs to be an entrepreneur in life.

- It takes time to build a network that produces residual income. Residual income is income that continues to be generated after the initial effort has been expended. One truly has to have endurance to run the race of network marketing.

34

BUSINESS NO-GO'S

This is my favorite business page, as I am an idea person. There were lots of ideas flowing daily. So many that it actually became frustrating, because we knew we couldn't get them all accomplished. And that meant missed learning opportunities and leaving money on the table. In the beginning, ideas were scarce, but once you start small and build, the floodgates open. I remember going to the library and checking out a book, Minding Your Own Business, by Raymond and Dorothy Moore, which changed our lives. Now we have so many ideas, some good and some not so good. Here are business ideas that were not so good, and never started, but you'll understand why.

LESSONS LEARNED:

- Little Rabbit Foo-Foo Birthday Parties: Little girls love dress-up parties, so why not offer a birthday party service where little girls are able to dress up live bunnies? We raised bunnies, and this is what happened in our home with our little girls. Why not spread the joy and let other little ones experience the same fun? OK, but what happens if the cute little bunny gets scared and scratches little Suzy or, worse yet, bites her? (Think lawsuits!) Or what if cute little Suzy hugs little rabbit Foo-Foo too tightly and she dies? (Think devastated child and owner.) Not starting this business saved us from a disastrous ending.

- Little Rabbit Poo-Poo Services: Rabbits make lots of poo, they just do. But the best part is that it is great fertilizer for gardens and houseplants, because it dries quickly, is non-odiferous, and is high in nitrogen and phosphorous. All those characteristics make it just right for houseplants. Our neighbor in the city came and asked to buy a bag of rabbit droppings for his garden and houseplants, and the million-dollar idea was born! Of course, it made perfect sense, as the product was free, plenteous, and never-ending. However, when I presented the idea to the two younger girls, they hated it. They were appalled at the thought and couldn't see beyond the public humiliation of marketing that type of product. Another idea down the pot...literally!

- Garage Sale Clean-up Crew: At the end of garage sales, people tend to be physically tired, tired of looking at their "stuff," and ready to have some free time. We would come in and clean up, haul away the leftovers, and put the garage back in functioning order. It would be perfect, as we would donate the unusable items to the thrift store, find free needed items for ourselves, and sell any "hot-sellers" on eBay. A win-win-win situation. My family did not go for it, as we did not have a pick-up and we lived in town and had nowhere to store the excess "stuff." Also, most garage sales end on weekends, and those days were our family rest days.

- Farmcation and Farm Camp: On our acreage we have an extra house that I wanted to purchase and rent out to families for farmcations and farm camp. The family did not go for it due to these reasons: What if the extra house was not rented year-round, and we had to pay two mortgages? What if the liability insurance was too high having visitors help on your farm? And then the safety issues of renting to strangers? Plus the risk of damage to the property? And of course, the extra time and work for upkeep on both properties. This idea was vetoed as too costly, too risky, and involving too many hours of work.

- Online scholarship business: The goal in our family is to graduate from college debt-free. To do this, the plan was to have college paid for by an outside source, such as community service or entrepreneurship scholarships, grants, the workplace, university athletic, academic or art scholarships, part-time jobs during college, or massive saving accounts. The goal was for Rachel to have an online scholarship service business during college, but there is a learning curve in college (literally!), and she found she didn't have the time. People will pay for your services in helping their child find money to pay for college. Navigating all the paperwork can be overwhelming and laborious, which is why there is a need for the Scholarship Tutor business.

- Beef Jerky Sales: My husband, Tim, loves beef jerky and created his own recipes for sweet and spicy and teriyaki jerky. Men tend to like beef jerky, and we found there was a demand for it. One needs quality meat, refrigeration space, and a dehydrator to make beef jerky. We thought of it as a possible business idea, but private parties cannot sell beef jerky in public, as it needs USDA approval. It is also time consuming, and ROI of time is hard to recoup. Our family eats the product before it gets in the bags! Save this idea for family and friends' gifts. There are too many regulations concerning meat products to make and sell jerky as a viable business. Save that idea for the meat lockers and the "big boys."

35

JOBS

Newspaper Routes
Greenhouse
Rogueing
Lifeguarding
Certified Nursing Assistant
Medication Aide
Dietary Aide
Coffee Shop Barista
Restaurant Worker
Vet Clinic Kennel Helper
ABA Therapy Tutor
Summer Camp Counselor/Wrangler
Fireworks Sales
Concrete Construction Crew
Assistant Manager
Live-in Nanny

LESSONS LEARNED:

- While owning businesses is ideal, being an employee can teach many skills, like pleasing a boss, being on time, having a good work ethic, being coachable, respectful, and trustworthy, and using great customer service. Also, being an employee can mean a steady paycheck to pay the bills while your child is getting their current venture up and running.

- I can't say enough about having a newspaper delivery route as a child. Warren Buffett started out with paper routes as a young boy. He juggled three different paper routes for two rival newspapers and spent the time thinking while he was working alone. Paper routes teach responsibility, reliability, organization, and a work ethic from a young age. Rachel and Christian started their first weekly paper route at seven and six years of age. Two years later, they added a daily route. It was great training for them, especially in customer service. They found that if they bent over backwards for the subscribers, the tips were plentiful, along with the treats. One nice "grandpa" on their route gave them money to buy dog food when he found out Rachel was delivering papers to buy her first dog. They also could compound their time by walking the dog they were dog sitting or pulling the child in the wagon they were babysitting while delivering papers.

- Acquisition of skills needs to be foremost on the mind when looking for a job for your children. What skills can they learn from this job that can be applied to future endeavors? Working in a greenhouse is a fantastic place to learn lifelong skills. The children now recognize plants, know how to landscape, plant, organize, care for plants, and clean up. They also learn customer service and how to use a cash register.

- Rogueing (working in the corn fields) teaches self-discipline, because the child will need to get up early and work in hot sweaty cornfields under less than ideal conditions. The child labor laws are different in each state, so check your state's laws, but in Nebraska a student can work at the age of 14 with limited hours and within a certain timeframe. An office job with air-conditioning is a piece of cake after working in the cornfields.

- Lifeguarding is one of those skills that can help your child find a job in many settings. It may not be the best paying, or the most stimulating, but being a lifeguard at an indoor pool during the off seasons, and at the outdoor pool during the warm seasons, makes for year-round employment. Summer camp lifeguard positions are plentiful, plus the CPR training is a universal skill.

- Obtaining a Nursing Assistant or Medication Aide certification not only helps the students find a job in the medical field, but it is also great preparation for the nursing field. Rachel is in nursing school, and her four years being a CNA in a nursing home have served her well. She is a kinesthetic learner, and working in the medical field prior to going to college gave her a great foundation. Working as a Dietary Aide in the nursing home is another skill set that will help in many fields. Not only did Christian honor the elderly, but he also learned about the medical field, food service, customer service, teamwork, and being orderly and efficient with his time.

- Experience as a coffee shop barista and a restaurant worker is life-long skill, where the young person finds out it is all about pleasing the customer. (Familiar theme with every job!) Specialty coffee shops are a hot industry right now, and that would enable Christian and Hannah to be able to work in almost any city. Amanya's experience working in a restaurant as a cashier, waiter, kitchen help, cook, and janitor has taught her many practical skills. Bottom line: it boils down to being able to take orders from a supervisor and having a great work ethic coming in to the job.

- A weekend kennel helper at the local vet clinic has been a great job for my daughters. Hannah and Amanya are responsible for caring for the boarded animals, the cleaning of the cages, administering needed medications, serving the customers, and following strict protocols. It exposes the child to the life of a veterinarian, veterinarian tech, dog groomer, and office help in a vet clinic. My daughter Hannah has a life-long love for horses, dogs, cats, goats, birds, and anything else that moves, flies, or slithers. It helped her immensely in deciding if she wanted to become a veterinarian.

- I cannot say enough about the merits of working in a summer camp setting. Whether it is working as a cabin counselor, on waterfront area, as a wrangler, as a lifeguard, as a kitchen helper, as a cook, or as a junior cabin leader—it is a plus for their character. Traditionally, summer camp jobs don't pay very well, but what the student gains in character development far outweighs the deficit in income. One of the most obvious benefits is being out in nature all summer and being grounded by nature. Taking care of campers who may be hot, overtired, homesick, or have emotional hurts adds to their resume of character traits quickly. If it is a faith-based camp, developing the spiritual aspect is the most important goal in life. All four of our children worked in a summer camp setting. Yes, income is needed in this world, but the monetary deficits are easily filled in. Character deficits are not. It takes purpose and time to develop one's character, and summer camp is a character incubator.

- Any reputable sales job will lead to life-long skills. As business owners, we have to be the best salespeople for our product or service business. And the best teacher is learning from the pros and emulating the masters. I purposefully choose mentors for my children who have great character, good business sense, and exemplary skills. I like to partner them with entrepreneurs who can light a fire down in their soul and continue to solidify the merits of being a business owner. One such local opportunity for my children has been in firework sales. The owner is a polished salesman with years of experience. He is a good teacher and the children absorbed his tutelage. Firework sales are only ten days during the year, but it is an intense, hot, and fun experience with valuable skills learned. Most of my children have had this experience, and it has only brought value to being an entrepreneur.

- Just as children need to start young and start small with their business ideas, so it is with their jobs. My son, at age 18, moved off the farm and left for the city lights. He was able to support himself, pay rent, and take care of his daily needs. He found stimulating jobs because of his many years of being responsible and making his own decisions. For 12 years he had been making decisions with his own businesses, which leads to being a bold and independent thinker, who is equipped with many viable skills to succeed in the work world. His first "real job" as a young adult was working on a concrete construction crew where they did pourings for new constructions. After a season, he concluded it was not a good fit for his skill set and moved on to a job as an assistant manager. At age 19, he was promoted to being an event manager, which utilized his strengths as a networker, salesman, people person, and one who gives attention to details.

- My oldest daughter served as a summer live-in nanny for a family with two young boys. Not only was she able to visit New York City weekly, but she was exposed to another culture, religion, region of the country, and parenting style. She gleaned valuable skills in caring for an infant, which helps in preparation for her career goal of working as a Neonatal Intensive Care Unit (NICU) nurse.

GARAGE SALES

BABY SITTING

ELDERLY SITTING

A'S AWESOME JEWELRY

SALES IN THE PIANO STUDIO

Resources

EntrepreneurShip Investigation (ESI)
esi.unl.edu

This is an exciting, interactive, and comprehensive curriculum project designed for youth, ages 10–19. ESI uses a variety of tools to help participants develop their entrepreneurial skills and find their business niche. Through exciting activities, case studies, and current technology, participants are transformed into budding entrepreneurs. (I have used this curriculum to train over 350 students since 2007.)

Who Owns the Ice House?
elimindset.com

Drawing on the entrepreneurial life lessons described in the book, *Who Owns the Ice House?* By Clifton Taulbert and Gary Schoeniger, the Ice House Entrepreneurship Program combines narrated chalkboard style presentations with video interviews and case studies featuring modern-day examples of entrepreneurs who have triumphed over adversity by embracing an entrepreneurial mindset. This program is powerful in its presentation and impact on future entrepreneurs as it targets the mindset and not just the how-tos. It gives a refreshing perspective on entrepreneurship. (I am a certified facilitator and highly recommend this program for teens and adults.)

Gallup:
gallupstrengthscenter.com/EP10

I highly recommend the EP10 for high school-aged students and above. It lists the top ten talents entrepreneurs need to survive and thrive. (I use this assessment tool with my high schoolers and adults.)

$100 Startup:
100startup.com

In The $100 Startup book, Chris Guillebeau shows you how to lead a life of adventure, meaning, and purpose—and earn a good living. (I really like this site, because it is simple, understandable, and doable. It is an "I can do this thing called entrepreneurship!" site.)

CEO Class:
effinghamceo.com

This is a model high school entrepreneurship program set up in local communities. It is one to implement in all our communities across the US. To start a CEO Class in your community, go to: midlandinstitute.com. It is a very impressive program for high schoolers.

Consortium for Entrepreneurship Education:
entre-ed.org

The Consortium for Entrepreneurship Education offers lists of classroom activities, youth entrepreneurship curriculum resources, case studies, classroom materials and products, and national conferences. (I attended two conferences in Charleston, SC, and Austin, TX. They provide valuable networking with other entrepreneurship educators.)

BizKid$:
bizkids.com

Biz Kid$ TV show educates children ages 6 to 12 about financial literacy, fiscal and social responsibility, work readiness, and entrepreneurship in a fun and memorable way. Videos, episodes, and lesson plans can be used on their own, or in combination with existing classroom curriculum. It's not hard to teach your students about money and business with Biz Kid$. (Our own children were featured on episode #406 in 2010.)

Business Opportunities Weblog:
business-opportunities.biz

If you need business ideas, franchise recommendations, stories of inventions, advice, a creativity boost, and more, Dane Carlson's site is the way to go. He has been blogging since 2001 and knows his stuff! It is very informative, and you can research for days on his site. Don't be put off by all the ads; dig and you will find gold, pure gold. (He interviewed me way back in 2004 for Simply Music piano lessons.)

How to Make Money as a Kid:
Howtomakemoneyasakid.com

Founder Steve L. Cooper's mission is to help kids reach their full potential early by helping them begin to earn money while they are still young. If kids will learn to take chances, work hard, and take the wins and losses as they come, they will have gained the refined skills to be ultra-successful, effective entrepreneurs by the time they become adults. (His site is contemporary, ever evolving, and has funny videos. Kids will enjoy them. Be sure to sign up for the 200 free biz ideas. His marketing is great.)

Books

Minding Your Own Business: A Common Sense Guide to Home Management and Industry, by Raymond and Dorothy Moore (We started with this book and used some of their business ideas. I highly recommend the wisdom and lifestyle taught in this book.)

Better than a Lemonade Stand!: Small Business Ideas for Kids, by Daryl Bernstein (I think Rachel took this book to bed with her in her early years!)

The Parents' Guide to Raising CEO Kids, by Dr. Jerry Cook and Sarah L. Cook (All four of our children were interviewed for this book. It contains over 100 inspiring testimonies from young entrepreneurs.)

Kidpreneurs: Young Entrepreneurs with Big Ideas, by Adam Toren and Matthew Toren (It gives a creative and humorous approach to teaching entrepreneurship and could be used in an elementary classroom setting.)

Young Bucks: How to Raise a Future Millionaire, by Troy Dunn (This is an easy read. Troy writes in a storyteller style and includes business ideas for kids.)

50 Money Making Ideas for Kids, by Lauree & L. Allen Burkett (We used this book also for ideas. It is a bit dated, but some business ideas are eternal.)

Make $1,000 in 35 Days, by Kandias Conda (This is a well-researched book chock full of resources. Take her challenge of making $1,000 in 35 days. It's a good discipline!)

More Business Ideas for Youth

1. Computer repair service
2. Handmade gifts
3. Gift wrapping services
4. Pet sitting services
5. Social media marketing online
6. Car and boat washing & detailing
7. Cookies and other baked goods
8. Techie device set up
9. Jewelry designing
10. Personal services
11. Handmade greeting cards
12. Poop handler for pets
13. Corner stands
14. Gift baskets
15. Upcycling old "stuff"
16. Become an online personality
17. Writing coach
18. Planning parties for children
19. Photography
20. Dog or cat treats
21. Online store

22. How-to videos
23. Garage sales
24. Invent something
25. The art collector
26. Clothing swap or consignment shop
27. Language / academic private tutoring
28. Music lessons
29. Post-construction cleanup
30. Holiday decorating
31. Lawn and snow care
32. Vegetable garden planting and maintenance
33. Professional blogging
34. Graphic designing
35. Freelance writing
36. Create and print custom t-shirts
37. Grow and sell organic vegetables, fruits, and herbs to restaurants
38. Sell on eBay
39. Sell used textbooks
40. Make gourmet jams, jellies, and sauces
41. Babysitting, chauffeuring, and tutoring
42. Recycle cans
43. Make dog or cat toys or personalized pet dishes
44. Make fruit, flower, or candy arrangements
45. Music practice buddy
46. Give musical instrument lessons
47. Make lip gloss or body lotions
48. Make hair scrunchies, ponytail holders, hair bows, and flowers

49. Knit scarves and hats
50. Make holiday ornaments.
51. Create scrapbooks or memory books
52. Make birdhouses / feeders
53. Make key chains or zipper pulls
54. Party server and cleaner-upper
55. Cooking classes with Kids
56. Video game rentals
57. Grow starter or house plants
58. House & plant sitting, check the mail, put out garbage, check pets
59. Packing (or unpacking) boxes for moving
60. Washing windows
61. Cleaning garages, basements, or storage spaces
62. Cleaning and organizing kitchen drawers
63. Cleaning pools
64. Spreading mulch
65. Painting mailboxes / fences
66. Making garden compost
67. Exercise buddy for kids
68. Being a nanny for a family
69. Helping with school projects
70. Painting faces at fairs
71. Spray painting crazy hair
72. Counseling at day camp
73. Babysitting
74. Parent's helper
75. Planning and entertaining at kids' birthday parties

76. Reading to kids
77. Entertaining kids after school
78. Tutoring help for kids
79. Refereeing or umpiring sports
80. Caddying for a golfer
81. Lifeguarding at a pool or beach
82. Creating websites
83. Researching (cell phones, gadgets, and others)
84. Marketing other people's products
85. Making web videos for business websites
86. Creating apps for Apple products
87. Cleaning RVs & campers
88. Parking cars for private parties (valet)
89. Being kids' chauffeur
90. Putting in docks in spring

Want Some Help?

Janita Pavelka offers several services that will help you implement entrepreneurship in your life and community:

- Coaching for community youth biz club leaders, either online or in person

- Coaching for parents, either online or in person

- Seminars on youth entrepreneurship

- Youth biz camps in your community

- Entrepreneurship workshops for adults or youth

- Entrepreneurship consultant services

For more information on her available programs and services, check out www.janitapavelka.com.

About the Author

Janita Pavelka is an award-winning entrepreneurship educator who believes that children and teens who develop their own businesses master real-life skills that can only be gained through doing. *Entrepreneuring* is a verb! These real-life skills include customer service, public speaking, problem solving, brainstorming, business and time management, a reason for doing the 3 R's, along with character-building traits. This is important, because building entrepreneurs is the backbone of our local, regional, national, and global economies.

Pavelka believes in a tri-fold approach to education, where students work on their businesses equal to their time spent in academic studies, along with weekly community service. Pavelka has a degree in Social Work/Psychology and Education, and she has been an educator for 26 years, teaching students from ages 4 to 91. She has been featured on TV and radio, in newspapers, magazines and blogs telling her family's story and spreading the message of youth entrepreneurship.

When not working to help grow businesses, she can be found spending time with her husband and four entrepreneurial children on Old MacDonald's farm living back to the basics and continuing to learn something new every day.

Acknowledgements

First of all, I want to acknowledge my parents, who raised us loving God, working hard, being respectful, and teaching resourcefulness. Mother and Dad, if you are the only ones who ever read this book, it is enough. I knew you would be proud, show the whole town, and it would brighten your world. Thank you for your unending support and for being the captains of my cheer team!

To my big sister Janel—Nel, I finally got 'er done. And if you would still be here on this earth, you would have made sure I finished it four years earlier! Thanks for always (well except for the cigar incident) being a great role model for me. You are missed deeply!

A big thanks goes to my husband, Tim, and our children, Greg, Rachel, Christian, Hannah, and Amanya, who challenge me to live with integrity, call me out when I don't, and accept me as a work in progress. Sorry, PavPack, you were my guinea pigs.

I want to thank my mentor, Roger Allmand, who speaks truth into my life, which motives me to take a risk and be faithful to my purpose on earth. You will never know your widespread influence on this world until Heaven.

To my friend who dreams with me, Robin Phipps. You are like my adult twin who believes in my dreams (and is not overwhelmed by them), who continues to encourage my kiddos, and whose very presence is motivation to excel.

A sweet thank you to Celeste Pierre, the creative illustrator of this book. You came into my life as a "special" piano student, and when our time together came to an end, I was left with an indelible mark of wonderment at the malleability of the human soul.

Lastly, this is for you, the one who is scared. The one who thinks, "I can't do it." The one who thinks, "I am not good enough." This book was five years in the making. It was written in the first year, spent four years of lying dormant under my bed, and then in the last year it underwent active editing. Don't do what I did. Push through your fears, take a risk, and don't worry about what other people think. A little bit every day is what will get you where you want to be. Don't listen to naysayers. Don't live by fear. "God has not given us a spirit of fear, but of power, of love and a sound mind." (2 Tim. 1:7). Be blessed, my friend.